The Financial Success Guide for Private Practice Optometrists

Written By P. Christopher Music, MBA

ISBN: 978-1-937205-21-8

Published by Sage Assets LLC, Florida, USA

Table of Contents

Introduction

As an optometrist in private practice for yourself, you've worked hard to build a solid reputation, a solid clientele and a solid practice. As you know, there are only so many hours each day. So how can you build and manage a practice and work hard to build a solid financial future as well?

Unfortunately, if you're not careful, all your hard work can still result in more loss than profit, more financial drain than gain; that's why you're here reading a book called *The Financial Success Guide for Private Practice Optometrists*. This book is an overview of the basic tools and procedures that a private practice professional would use to maximize his or her economic well-being and quality of life.

This summary is distilled from decades of research and experience in the area of personal economics and finance and gives the reader a direct solution for handling any area of financial duress or improving one's general financial condition.

You work hard to build a practice you can be proud of; however, taking care of your personal finances as well can become a full-time job! It doesn't have to be—this guide can help!

In **Chapter 1**, we discuss what we call the "barriers to prosperity." In order to get an understanding of how to achieve financial prosperity, success, and abundance as a private practice owner, we first must understand and delineate exactly what we're up against in our modern economy.

Chapter 2 focuses on the engine to your wealth: your clinic. Since it is (or should be) the largest and riskiest asset you own, it is imperative that you not only maximize the gross income of your practice but also the gross profit. There are 8 major areas that determine the gross income and profit in an optometry clinic and we'll cover those in detail.

Chapter 3 is called "Your Household is a Business" for one very good reason: it is! In much the same way you learn to gain greater control over your practice finances in chapter 2, you will learn to do the same for your household financial situation in this chapter.

This is not an either/or situation, but a both/and scenario and you'll find that once your practice and home finances are in order, you can safely put them on "autopilot" and focus on what matters most: your professional and personal satisfaction.

Chapter 4 covers what it means to be a financial advisor in general, and what financial planning means for you, specifically. Many of us know financial advisors, but what exactly do they do and how they can help us? Once and for all, this chapter on financial planning clears it all up for you. Plus you'll get a FREE interview worksheet to download to help you in your search for the "Ideal Financial Advisor".

Chapter 5 gets very specific with something called "The 9 Elements of a Financial Plan for a Private Practice Optometrist." Here you'll discover a step-by-step plan that will help you tackle such financial topics as "planning for income," "policies and procedures" and "debt and credit" management, and more.

Chapter 6 asks about your end-game: the Exit Plan. What is your plan to transition out of the practice? How will you do it? Will it be for maximum value? These questions are explored to orient you to your inevitable exit and how to make the most out of it—beginning with the end in mind.

Finally, **The Bonus Section** asks the question, *"What's next?"* What's next for you, for your practice, for your business and personal finances? We'll answer that question with something called the Financial Prosperity Index® assessment.

This diagnostic tool was created to demonstrate to a professional how financially prosperous and secure they are in their current financial condition compared to the Optimum Financial Condition for any household. This tool will help you assess where you are today and help you identify areas of weakness and strengths so you can take immediate action in the areas that are in critical condition needing improvement. *This is where you begin to truly understand how you will achieve your financial goals.* Visit **www.FinancialProsperityIndex.com** to take this assessment.

You work hard, so it is our mission to create a short, simple, jam-packed resource with this guide that will help you achieve your financial goals as a private practice optometrist. With that in mind, let's forge ahead to **Chapter 1:** *The Barriers to Prosperity.*

Chapter 1

The Barriers to Prosperity

Before starting any journey, it's important to make sure the route you're ready to travel is free of obstacles, debris, potholes, roadblocks and other assorted barriers to your progress.

Likewise, before we undertake this journey to create a more financially responsible, ultimately more successful you, it is important to identify the barriers to prosperity that, like potholes, promise to give you a bumpy ride if you don't; a) spot them early on, and b) take great pains to avoid them as they approach.

To say that we are working harder and making less these days is, perhaps, the understatement of the year. Often we tend to blame this on some blanket excuse like "the economy," but it is more than just one central barrier impeding our success. In fact, there are several factors that are working against us every day, whether we're actually aware of them or not.

So while the economy may be a prohibiting factor, so are other "barriers to your prosperity" like bad advice, taxes and even lack of education to name a few. Over the years we have identified, analyzed and catalogued nine common barriers, each of which we cover comprehensively in this chapter.

Much as potholes on a road trip mess with our shocks or detours send us off track, the nine barriers actively prevent us from achieving the success and abundance we seek for taking the risks associated with being private practice owners.

There is a continual flow of economic factors that will carry one downstream and over the waterfall unless one swims against the current. If you want to get upstream, then you are going to have to know something about the river and you're going to have to know how to swim.

Let's clarify exactly what's briskly taking us downstream:

The 1st Barrier to Prosperity: *Lack of Education*

It might sound like an insult, at first, to suggest that "lack of education" is a potential problem for you. After all, as an optometrist you have been very well educated in your field of study and the different aspects of patient treatment. You are able to provide quality services as a result of the high level of technical training you've received during your career. You rightfully expect to be able to have a successful clinic based on the quality of the work that you do. But, as you've no doubt experienced, delivering quality patient treatment is only part of the equation.

If you're going into private practice there is another function that you have to know in addition to your field of expertise—how to run a business. The problem is most of us were never taught how to run a business—not in our clinical studies, certainly not in our medical studies and, oftentimes, not even in our business studies (if we've even followed that course track). In fact, even if we have minored—or majored—in business we're often unprepared come graduation day.

What about your education in personal finance over the years? Did you learn about money management in elementary or middle school? High school? College or grad school? No? The subject of personal economics is not taught in any educational curriculum unless you are training to be a financial planner. This is a glaring omission in your understanding of the subject and this translates into the financial condition of your household, whether acceptable or not.

The good news is it's never too late to learn! Fortunately, education is readily available on how to function and operate as a successful practice owner. Books, courses, seminars, even software is available to help you run your business smoothly. Just as important, however, there is education that exists on the correct tools and techniques to actually build wealth safely.

The 2nd Barrier to Prosperity: *False Information*

We all want to make the right choices when it comes to the financial decisions that affect our practices, our lives and particularly our bank accounts. In order to do that, we have to rely on certain information and what we believe to be factual in order to make correct decisions. But, who has the correct information? *Bloomberg Television? Money Magazine? USA Today?*

Or how about a financial advisor, accountant, next door neighbor, or brother-in-law? Unfortunately, there is WAY MORE incorrect information out there about your finances than there is correct information. The problem is that we often cannot distinguish between what is true and what is not.

How can you tell? Here's the one "true" answer: **the results**!

What financial condition are you in right now? If you are having good results, then you are likely using correct information. If your results are less than optimum, then the information is incorrect. Believe it or not, that is the simplicity of the matter.

The 3rd Barrier to Prosperity: *Bad Advice*

Money is a lot like math; people either "get it" or they don't. Of course, that is why financial advisors exist;

to give advice and make recommendations for people who "don't get it" because they do.

As a result of "not getting it," many people will simply decide that the financial area is something that cannot be understood so they will rely solely on somebody else to advise them on what to do.

While this is certainly legal, it is also rather dangerous. Merely handing over your financial dealings to a complete stranger, regardless of the degrees on his or her wall, deprives you of certainty and confidence regarding whether the advice that you are receiving is appropriate or not.

Bad financial advice can come from anywhere—financial professionals, family, friends, self-help gurus, teachers, etc. Results of bad advice can include such errors as bad investment timing or picking the wrong stocks or mutual funds, improper purchases and tax problems, not to mention spending a whole bunch of time and effort with nothing to show for it.

The financial industry is full of competent advisors who diligently work in their client's best interest. However, there are some advisors who really shouldn't be involved in the business in the first place. Moreover, there are many non-professionals who love to give their own opinions, only they are not experiencing the Optimum Financial Condition in their own lives.

The key for you is to discern from whom you should be taking your advice.

The 4th Barrier to Prosperity: *Inflation*

Inflation is created solely by the fact that we use a debt-based monetary system. All of the currency that we use to pay for and purchase goods and services is loaned into existence through our banking system. Since interest is charged and can only be paid by the same currency that is borrowed into existence in the first place, more currency must be borrowed to satisfy the debt. Therefore, more money must be created without a corresponding increase in the value of goods and services in the economy.

In short, and without all the technical jargon, inflation is simply too much money in the nation trying to match up with too few goods and services. It appears that **prices are going up**, but in actuality, the **value of the dollar is simply declining**. The value of the service or the good stays the same. Therefore, inflation is the greatest long-term threat to your wealth that you will face the rest of your life. Since the only value money has is its ability to be exchanged for the goods and services we need, the problem of inflation will have to be solved for you individually.

The 5th Barrier to Prosperity: *Taxes*

Government has the power to tax your income, the transfer of your estate and even your ability to give gifts to others, among a host of other goods and services. However, the payment of income, estate and gift taxes are to some degree voluntary.

The Internal Revenue Code is designed to reward those who go to the effort to arrange their financial affairs in a certain manner and to penalize those who are ignorant and seek simplicity. Every dollar paid to the government is one less dollar allocated to your family's most valued goals and objectives, so it is therefore imperative that a strategy to keep one's tax liabilities to a minimum be implemented.

In short, one of the best ways to make money without actually earning any additional income is to save money. The best place to start saving money is by learning how to manage your taxes in a way that is more beneficial to you than to the government.

The 6th Barrier to Prosperity: *Financial Predators*

As a professional in our society, particularly in the medical field, you are inevitably perceived to be "affluent" or "wealthy," whether or not it's true. If you appear successful, it will be presumed that you *are* successful. As the society we live in moves more and more toward a welfare state (taking from those who produce and giving it to those who don't) and desperate people realize that they cannot make it economically on their own, they will seek to find it from others, namely through a favorite pastime—lawsuits.

According to some reports, approximately 50,000 lawsuits are filed every day in this country (that's one every 2 seconds!) and there is no penalty for filing a lawsuit and not winning. While many of these suits have merit, many more do not. we cannot imagine working to accumulate assets and own them in such a way as to leave them open to adverse judgments, yet most professionals are overwhelmingly and unknowingly exposed to this threat on a daily basis. Doing your homework to avoid threat from financial predators is a must in today's litigious society.

The 7th Barrier to Prosperity: *Excessive Regulation*

Our government does one thing very well: solve the problem of a few bad apples by monitoring the activities of everyone. In short, thanks to the fraudulent, negligent or even culpable actions of a rare few in your profession (and others), over-regulation is a problem all professionals face, especially those in private practice.

The costs of compliance go up while the rates you need to charge your clients become too expensive for them. The result is, of course, more hours and more headaches for less pay. Unless your practice can run profitably in spite of these extraneous burdens, you have little chance of achieving your goals.

The 8th Barrier to Prosperity: *Debt*

Buy now, pay later!

Whether we like it or not, the fact is we live in a society that believes that credit equals money—but nothing could be further from the truth. "Money" is a unit of value that represents goods and services. "Credit" is the borrowing of these units. According to recent research, the average American household has over $90,000 in household debt, including mortgages.

This is actually a financial catastrophe! However, this is considered "normal" since virtually everyone we know spends more than they earn. In short, the general public seems to feel, "Everyone else is doing it, so why can't I?"

When we choose to enrich the banking institutions rather than our own households, we should not then be surprised when we end up poor after a lifetime of work. Solving this threat to your wealth is completely within your control and must be handled if you want to enjoy long-term prosperity.

The 9th Barrier to Prosperity: *Human Behavior*

As modern humans we are intelligent beings, capable of the creation of incredible things. At the same time, we sometimes act in irrational ways that are counter to all logic or intelligent sensibility. This can be summed up in a relatively new field of research called "Behavioral Finance."

There are certain emotional reactions that can be counted upon in the area of finances for most people: procrastination in getting things done (i.e. paying bills, mailing off the taxes, etc.), greed and fear when it comes to managing investments, taking advice from unqualified people and making excuses for no results, to name a few. These emotional responses are some of the most insidious barriers to your own success. Fortunately, they are often the ones that you are most able to control—and rectify.

Parting Words about the Barriers to Prosperity

As you read this book, there is a river of societal and economic factors that are negatively affecting you and carrying you downstream **whether you like it or not**. If you do nothing, it will carry you downriver and over the waterfall.

Even if you choose to act, you must act in the right way to reverse the flow. If you act erratically without coordination of action and use of correct procedures, for instance, you will wear yourself out and will wind up over the waterfall anyway. Only by using a coordinated plan of action with efficient techniques and tools to move yourself up the river will you finally arrive at your dual destination: a safe port and an enjoyable trip.

That is what this book is all about; handling these nine barriers to prosperity so that you can get ahead financially by being efficient and effective in your financial life.

Now, it's on to the next leg of our journey...

Chapter 2

Prosperity in Your Practice— 6 Fundamental Metrics to Measure the Productivity and Profitability of Your Clinic

Is your practice prosperous? It's a question we should be asking more often. The question is not: is your practice surviving? It's not a matter of your practice breaking even. If you are only surviving and/or breaking even, you can be doing better. And if you are doing well, you can always do better.

Prosperity is a goal for all, but for many of us it may feel like an unreachable goal. This chapter addresses six simple things you can start measuring to ensure that your practice isn't just surviving, but prospering.

You can't manage what you don't measure. When running an optometry practice there are certain rules-of-thumb, or metrics, one should be using to determine how well the practice is performing.

But before we dig into specific metrics regarding practice performance, we must look at how a practice should be operating if it was affluent and expanding and at the top of its class—the elite practice.

While we can certainly write a whole book answering that one question about practice prosperity, for the sake of simplicity we will look at the major areas that will make you or break you as far as gross income and profit is concerned.

Marketing

This is a critical control point in your income because you want your current and new patients to bond to your practice. Marketing is such an important part of your practice, and if done correctly, can create a fortune for the owner. A proper understanding and application of these tools is necessary for success.

The elite practice:

- ✓ Would be visible to its public and participating in community activities.
- ✓ Maintains a database of both current and prospective patients and sends regular mailings to them.
- ✓ Routinely collects emails from all patients and a monthly e-newsletter is consistently sent.
- ✓ Has an increasing internet presence through the use of interactive websites, additional email marketing programs, social media and patient reviews.
- ✓ Has one person assigned marketing manager responsibilities and spends no less than 5 hours a week promoting the practice.

- ✓ Creates promotional and branding materials for new and repeat business based on patient surveys and feedback.
- ✓ Has an abundance of new and returning patients coming into the practice on a weekly basis.
- ✓ Has the source of all new patients tracked and that information would be used to create promotional programs for new patients.

Patient Treatment

The quality of your patient care and how effectively you sell treatment plans determines your success in this area of your practice. Your Revenue Per Exam (RPE) rises when you are successful in selling treatment plans. However, as you gain more patients, your selling time is typically overwhelmed by patient treatment, causing a lowered RPE and viability issues. This is handled by the proper organization of your group for improved profitability.

The optimal practice:

- ✓ Would have superlative patient care.
- ✓ Experiences very low cancellation rates (< 5%).
- ✓ Has virtually all patients accepting the recommended treatment plans for their eye care and seeing them through to completion.
- ✓ Has the staff using time to improve their technical skills or promoting the practice when cancellations do occur.

- ✓ Objectively measures each clinician's technical performance and holding it to a very high standard.
- ✓ Has patients who happily return for their annual eye exam and who acquire the recommended purchases.
- ✓ Would be making quality control follow-up calls to gain feedback on patient services.
- ✓ Has the doctor and staff improving quality of care through continuing education.
- ✓ Has a dedicated person who completes the financial arrangements of the treatment plan.

Patient Scheduling

Scheduling control is the area that will make or break your practice. Significant lost income can be recovered by a standard scheduling protocol. Improving your control over this area can have a significant impact on the profitability of your practice, especially in solving the problem of who does the scheduling and how.

The elite practice:

- ✓ Would be in total control of patient scheduling, ensuring that holes in the schedule are filled.
- ✓ Has the staff aggressively making sure that patients are keeping their appointments and the receptionist always confirming the next appointment of each patient as they leave the practice.

- ✓ Has a policy of re-confirming those patients that miss appointments.
- ✓ Knows exactly what the cancellation rate is and how much money is lost per week due to those cancellations.
- ✓ Provides necessary resources within the practice to handle the increased patient load as the schedule gets busier with higher patient visits.
- ✓ Consistently has staff doctors on time for their patient appointments.
- ✓ Enjoys a smooth schedule—one not subject to the roller-coaster effect.
- ✓ Has a precise and coordinated activation program in place to ensure that an optimum number of patients are scheduled for recommended services.

Billing and Collections: *Planning for Future Income*

This is an area which is usually deficient in a typical optometry practice. Proactive planning for future income is the hallmark of any successful professional practice. The truth is that all income is made because it was planned for, even if it seems like your income is the result of unpredictable events. Much can be done in this area to create a greater gross income for the practice and a greater profit margin for the owners such as getting control over billing and collections actions and intelligent investment in money-making assets.

The successful practice:

- ✓ Would have an extremely efficient system of working out the financial arrangements before treatment is performed and accounts would be followed up to ensure payment is made.
- ✓ Would know exactly how much is invoiced and collected each week.
- ✓ Would have a high level of prediction of future income and would not be experiencing any cash flow problems while paying the owners a consistent salary or draw.
- ✓ Accounts receivable would always be declining or non-existent.
- ✓ Has correct and readily available financial statements for the practice owner at any time.
- ✓ Has proper coding for maximum reimbursement and minimal denials with an effective system for refiling claims, if needed.
- ✓ Would collect all co-pays and deductibles without exception on the day of visit.
- ✓ Experiences a constantly improving Revenue Per Exam statistic, providing more profit for the owners of the practice.

Patient Referrals

This is a huge and largely untapped goldmine in your practice but very easy to improve. Happy patients are willing to refer if you just ask them. Mastering this area can really expand a practice and your income if you integrate the promotion of referrals into your daily marketing activities.

The excellent optometry practice:

- ✓ Will continually ask patients to refer their friends and family and will provide them with brochures, information packets, online resources and referral cards for this purpose.
- ✓ Teach every referring patient exactly what to do to refer new patients to the practice.
- ✓ Acknowledges every patient when a referral is made.
- ✓ Has an increasing general trend of patient referrals.
- ✓ Knows who the top five referring patients are and has the staff work to support their referral activities.
- ✓ Promotes the importance of referrals in all of its marketing materials and the entire staff promotes referrals in their daily work.
- ✓ Surveys patients for their opinions and feedback.
- ✓ Would have an online presence that would stimulate referrals through videos, testimonials and other informational tools to register new patients.

Personnel Efficiency

Many of us do not hire people who are proven to be productive and once we hire them we spend too little time training them to succeed on their new job. This applies to new doctors or the administrative staff. A practice that is growing will likely need to hire a new doctor. Weakness in your ability to pick the correct candidate and train them to be productive will greatly inhibit your practice's viability. This also applies to hiring and training your administrative staff. An untrained receptionist who cannot get patients to keep their appointments or collect all the money due across the desk is worthless to you even if she can do everything else. An inefficient staff only makes YOU work that much harder.

The elite practice:

- ✓ Would be experiencing expansion in gross income as well as take-home pay due to the competence and productivity of each of its staff members.
- ✓ Trains all of the staff in clinical and administrative functions on an ongoing basis.
- ✓ Has each doctor complete patient records before moving on to the next patient and has all other administration of the practice well-organized.
- ✓ Affords the owner a position where he/she would not be taking work home and would not have to check in when on vacation or away from the practice, knowing that the work is getting completed correctly.
- ✓ Enjoys smooth management since all staff members would be doing their jobs expertly and as a team.

Stress

Owning and running a private practice can be a challenge. Working with staff, patients, regulators, vendors and others can take a toll on one's outlook and relationships with family and friends. It is true that the more one enjoys what he does, the more successful he will be. However, some situations can put one on an emotional rollercoaster, creating worry and anxiety from stressors such as debt, low income, problematic personnel and patients or regulatory threats.

The optimum practice:

- ✓ Would have an environment where the stress is quite low and morale is high.
- ✓ Has a productive group where everyone has the intention of expanding a successful practice and deriving the personal satisfaction of a job well done.
- ✓ Has the owner looking forward to going into work every day and excited about future plans.
- ✓ Is where everyone is having FUN.

If this is not what your practice looks like, then you are losing a fortune in lost income due to unnecessary stressful factors.

Management Principles

A business must be managed by someone who knows what they are doing. A person who runs a business is known as an executive or manager and has tools of the trade just like the methods you use to treat patients in optometry medicine. The successful practice owner knows and uses these tools and techniques; the unsuccessful one does not. There aren't any other explanations.

The elite practice:

- ✓ Makes abundant gross income and operates in the upper tenth in profitability compared to other professional practices in its industry.
- ✓ Acts as a cohesive team where the mission and goals of the practice are known and agreed-upon by all staff members and patients.
- ✓ Has an excellent credit rating.
- ✓ Enjoys increasing profits and income.
- ✓ Has enough cash reserves to handle periods of low income, avoiding the cycle of boom and bust that often happens with a small business.
- ✓ Derives the most value from all assets and personnel in the practice.
- ✓ Operates on merit, where the more productive staff members are rewarded with a standard and known bonus system.

Owning an elite practice is much more fun and interesting than struggling with the multitude of problems that manifest at the low end of the scale in each of these areas. We think you'll agree you would prefer to own a successful business rather than an unsuccessful one.

Now that we know what an elite clinic would look like, we can compare our current state of operation to determine what needs to be done to attain that higher status.

The Six Fundamental Metrics

You were never trained in optometry school how to run a company or understand the concept of Return on Investment (ROI); these six fundamentals will bridge that gap to make you successful and prosperous.

Now let's take a look at some of the metrics that will measure our ascent to the elite status of private practices:

Fundamental Number 1:

You Should be Taking Home at Least 35% of Your Gross Income.

The main financial purpose of private practice is to make a profit without the "glass ceiling" of a corporate overseer giving you pre-set limits. You are, in fact, an entrepreneur and should, in fact, be thinking like one. Embrace that entrepreneurial spirit!

To gauge your level of prosperity, a well-run optometry practice should permit the owners to take home just over one-third of the gross income on an annual basis. That means if you are generating $600,000 in gross income, then you should ultimately bring home more than $210,000 in salary and profits.

This may seem high. But it's actually not. Still, the average household is taking home much less than that. This number is based on a practice that has a very healthy mix of both eye and medical exams. As you derive more income from the medical side of the practice, your cost of goods is pushed downward. Because of the low overall expense to provide medical services, this higher profit margin is blended with the optical side to create a higher net profit and take home income.

Another factor that has a huge impact of profitability is management. If there are profitability issues, then one reason is that the average private practice is not utilizing a proven business management system. In the typical scenario, we build and grow our practices and everything seems fine until we suddenly notice a drop-off or leveling in profits. Our expansion hits a wall and rather than doing the standard actions with personnel, marketing, financial management, etc., we look for "tips and tricks" from our peers to help instead of a coordinated system. These "emergency" measures are implemented to make more money until the next "emergency" appears—and on it goes for a lackluster career in private practice.

This haphazard approach ends up costing much more in lost profits than it ever would to pay the consultant fees. If the consultant was a good one, the return on investment would be much more than the cost anyway—and this would be most noticeable in your bottom line.

For example, let's say you paid a consultant $30,000 for consulting you on proven practice management techniques. Over one year, you experienced an additional

$60,000 in gross income. That is a 100% profit in one year to your practice and will repeat itself year after year from now on. There is no other investment that gets those kinds of results. This is the number one reason why practices do not reach their potential. You were never trained in optometry school how to run a company or understand the concept of Return on Investment (ROI); these seven fundamentals will bridge that gap to make you successful and prosperous.

Fundamental Number 2:
The Average Revenue Per Exam Should Exceed $310.

The average optometry practice should be generating at least $310 in Revenue Per Exam. This is actually a national average but can, and should, be higher than that.

This is done by providing a thorough exam—collecting ALL of the data about the patient in the pre-test, including information about potential medical conditions, lifestyle, and other potential areas to address.

This figure is also determined by how well the practitioner and all support staff communicate the value of optometry services to the public to get them to demand what they actually need. For example, does the patient need safety glasses? A second pair of glasses at home? Glasses for using the computer at work, or while driving? Does he need sunglasses? Extra contacts? Are there any other potential needs?

One of the best ways to ensure that nothing is missed in the exam is to have a checklist of questions to ask or information to collect that is designed to standardly create a thorough and pleasant exam experience for both the staff and the patient. Set it up so that every necessary line of questioning is prompted and nothing is missed. If the questionnaire is completed fully each and every exam, then all of the present and future needs of the patient will be known and proper follow-up can occur. Lost revenue from missing sales opportunities can be eliminated if this process is embedded into your daily routine.

Fundamental Number 3:

No More Than 22% of Gross Income Should be Going to Employee Salaries and Benefits.

As we do financial planning for our optometrist clients, we often find that they will pay their staff well and deprive themselves of the fruits of private practice ownership. It is known that a happy staff is a productive staff, but what's the point if they're not working for a prosperous owner?

All investments within a business must make a profit: this includes marketing, property, equipment and staff. When any of these areas do not produce to their greatest potential, other productive areas in the practice attempt to make up for those inefficiencies and the general activity becomes less profitable.

The bottom line is this: If more than 22% of your gross income is going to staff salaries and benefits, then something is wrong with the business model and it needs to be fixed in order to produce more profit. You either have too many people on staff or they are not producing at a profitable enough level to justify the expense. A thorough review of your salary expenses compared to the gross income generated by each staff member can help sort this out.

Fundamental Number 4:

More than 25% of Total Office Visits Should be Medical Visits.

Any optometry practice can focus on delivering any service for which the doctor and staff is trained to deliver. And, as with any professional practice, there are some deliverable services that are more profitable than others.

The medical visit is simply more profitable than the optical visit. If you have been trained on how to deliver certain medical services, it makes sense to deliver those instead of outsourcing them to an ophthalmologist since they can be done cost-effectively.

This may be a new way of thinking if you have built your existing practice on providing optical exams and follow-up services. If this is the case, look for ways to position your practice to deliver on the medical side. Adjust your marketing and promotion to reflect this advance in your clinic's services. Build referral activities that focus on attracting patients that need medical services that fit your skill set.

If you can create a practice where more than 25% of your total office visits are medical in nature, you should experience a significant increase in your gross income and profit.

Fundamental Number 5:

Over 70% of Your Patients Should Be Returning for Their Annual Preventative Eye Exam.

Preventative eye care is a necessity for an optometry practice. We all know that already. However, the public is given the idea that they only need an exam every other year because that is what the insurance companies will reimburse. This type of marketing is tough to overcome because the public has been indoctrinated into the idea that insurance will pay for everything.

Promoting annual eye exams not only sustains a practice but it is also a needed public service. With the equipment available today, problems with the eyes can be detected early and treated before they become full-scale emergencies. This reality has to be promoted more effectively than the perception grooved in by the insurance industry.

A campaign promoting the value of an annual exam should be undertaken to communicate to all of your patients, past and present. The annual exam could be positioned as an annual "verification" that everything is good or could be done to create awareness of some new affliction. Either way, a continuing promotional effort is needed to keep your patient demanding preventative eye care.

One of the most effective ways to support this campaign is to write a weekly blog or article that is then placed into your social media profiles and email marketing blasts. Tell stories about how a person's sight was saved from early detection. Show case studies and statistics. And so on... The more your patients hear from you regarding your expertise and recent developments and discoveries in your field, the more they will be aware of the benefits of good vision in the living of their lives.

Fundamental Number 6:

You Should be Spending About 5% of the Gross Income of the Practice on Marketing Expenses.

We know that marketing is the lifeblood of a business and, as a private practice optometrist, it is the difference between a robust, booming company and one that whimpers along until the doors close.

Here is the typical scenario: You need new patients, so you promote and spend money on marketing activities.

When done correctly, these programs create a host of new patients who come in the door. Everything is fine now since there are a lot of patients to treat—that is, until they complete their treatment programs. Income then slumps, and a whole new surge of marketing activity ensues. New patients come in, income goes back up, and the cycle of boom and bust continues on and on.

The only way to break this rollercoaster ride is to actively market your practice constantly regardless of the number of patients you are treating.

The first action is to perform an analysis of your marketing programs. This would be a breakdown of the cost versus the income generated by each marketing campaign. When you determine which programs generate the greatest return on investment, those efforts would then be strengthened. Any program not earning a decent rate of return is then discontinued.

The next action is to allocate money every month toward the most profitable and effective marketing campaigns. How much should you allocate each month? Around 5% of gross income.

This allocation would be done after paying yourself first but before paying rent, salaries, and other monthly bills. It should also be accounted for separately so that it isn't erroneously spent on something else.

You see, without a constant marketing and promotional effort, you will not have a constant flow of patient visits to expand the practice. This leads to overpaying for staff and overhead and a vaporization of your profits, not to mention the emotional rollercoaster ride.

Part of the marketing effort is the establishment of a killer referral system. For a professional practice, 70% of your patients should come from referrals. But, you must be referable. That means that you have your marketing materials in such a state so that your credibility shines through and that your patients know to use them with their circle of influence. This is how you separate yourself from the competition.

In our experience working with optometrists, this is truly one of the major differences between a stable, profitable and expanding practice and one that isn't.

Parting Words about Prosperity in Your Practice

I have summarized here just six of the many standard metrics that should be used in a practice to measure its production and profitability. Obviously, there are more ways to measure productivity for your practice, as well as ways to increase profitability if you find your numbers lacking. The goal is to personalize these methods and put them into practice sooner rather than later. If you don't like the measurements you're taking, don't stop measuring; just start producing better numbers to measure! After all, your practice is your key to financial prosperity at home—the engine that provides the money to help you achieve your life goals.

If your practice doesn't work for you, then by default you work for it and it will consume you if not controlled, measured and molded to suit your needs. Hopefully, these six simple measurement tips give you some insight on how to improve the quality of your practice and make your participation in it much more enjoyable.

Chapter 3

Your Household is a Business

Businesses exist for one primary purpose: to provide a product or service to someone else in exchange for the money it needs to survive. No matter the business, the industry or the niche market you serve, a business is a business is a business. From Microsoft to the Red Cross, from Pier 1 Imports to the Catholic Church, ALL businesses exist **to provide a product or service to someone else in exchange for the money it needs to survive**.

Just look at your business. You provide treatment to patients in your practice in exchange for money and goodwill and you have a whole system set up to efficiently deliver those services in a way that ensures nothing interferes with the money flow. The practice must be profitable to continue to exist and provide service.

Too Few Practitioners Treat Their Home Like a Business

Your household is really no different from your clinic. Think about it: your household has income, expenses, assets and liabilities—just like any other business. It has a tax ID number, otherwise known as your social security number. It has a "staff" (anyone who lives there) that provides products or services (your jobs).

While they may reside in the corner bedroom instead of the corner office, the household "executives"—you, or you and your spouse—ultimately own all of the assets and debts of the household including all or part of the professional practice, the real estate, retirement accounts, bank accounts and everything else.

All of the profits and losses flow up from all of these assets into the household, and every year it provides an accounting of all of its economic activity in the form of an income tax return. The government views your household as a business; you should, too. In fact, the sooner you treat your home like a business, one with the intention to make a profit, the more quickly you will see better results from your financial planning activities.

CFO: Your Name Goes Here

Every business needs a Chief Financial Officer, the CFO. This is the person who is ultimately responsible for the financial condition of the business, whether good, bad or ugly. This must be done by one person, never by committee, because compromised agreement will always be financially disastrous for a company. There's a reason it's called "death by committee" (has a committee ever decided anything?).

Instead, every household must have **only one person** who is ultimately responsible for the economic condition of the family unit. He or she will have the final decision on how the family's money will be managed and spent, even if most decisions are made jointly. And that person must have an understanding of how finance and economics works, or the group will destroy itself under debt and waste.

Many CFOs have no problem working double-time to understand the finances that surround their business model, and yet act irrationally—even irresponsibly—concerning their household finances. If you are finding yourself lacking in your household CFO duties, bone up; get informed, get educated, read books, take online classes or join local seminars until you are confident you can meet the job requirements!

The Profitable Household is a Happy Household

Now, it's one thing to run your household like a business but the real question becomes: **Are you running your household business profitably**? What is the profit margin of the household? In other words, what is the percentage of the income that is not spent on expenses? How much is saved in accounts that can be accessed at a future point in time? 10%? 20%? 30%?

If your practice is operating at a 20% profit margin (let's say $500,000 gross income with $100,000 net income), then your household should have a profit margin as well (for example, $20,000 saved from $100,000 take home income) ***at the very least.*** Ideally, it actually should be **much, much higher** than that, but we'll start here.

If it's not there yet, take steps to get it there. For instance, if you're only saving $5,000 per year but still making 100 grand, on what are you spending the rest? Where are you "leaking money," as they say?

One of the best ways to be a more effective CFO is not only making more money but also finding ways to get more value out of the money you spend.

The House Where Profit Lives

Before determining how wealthy you are, you have to define what "profit" means to you. Yes, we all want to spend less than we make, but while your household has many similarities to your business, there are critical differences.

Take a look at your household finances right now. How would you describe your current financial situation?:

- Are you affluent?
- Middle class?
- Barely breaking even?
- Drowning in debt?

A good perspective is to ask yourself, "Would I run my household the way I currently do if the intent was to make a profit?" And what is the profit? Remember, when it comes to your household, profit isn't always listed in dollars and cents.

Educated children, a nice home, time to pursue your dreams, comfortable lifestyle, plenty of money set aside as a cushion for life's uncertainties... these are all profitable returns on your investment.

Parting Words about Your Household; The Parent Company

Our clients are often perplexed when we ask them to treat their home like a business, and their reaction is certainly understandable. For years we have been taught to keep "business" and "personal" separate.

But as our work- and home-lives continue to blend and merge, with more hours spent on the job than at home and, increasingly, many business owners treating the den or spare bedroom as a "home office," it only makes sense to begin treating the home like a business.

When it comes to your household finances, in particular, of course you'll agree that treating your home like a business only makes sense; it is the parent company into which all profits from your investments flow. As humans we like to keep things separate; work and play, church and state, household expenses and business expenses. But now more than ever it is vital that you begin to address your household income with the same veracity, rationale and professionalism as you do your business income.

The surest way to offset business gain is by losses at home. The goal is to strive for "balance" in all things, and your household and business finances are no different. Only when your business and home financial spreadsheets "balance" will both be able to flourish.

Chapter 4

What is Financial Planning Anyway?

We often take the term "financial planning" for granted, assuming that just because we hear it all the time we understand its many and various aspects. However, the term "financial planning" is often misunderstood because it is a relatively new profession. Here's an example...

Once upon a time people had accountants, stock brokers, bankers and attorneys who operated independently and autonomously, never consulting with each other regarding mutual clients. As times advanced, new laws were enacted and financial issues became increasingly complicated. The demand for something more multi-faceted than these distinctly separate professions grew as well. The solution was to combine insurance, investment, tax, banking and legal professions into a more unified, coordinated whole—a process that is continuing today.

We all seem to know someone who calls him—or herself a "financial planner"—the life insurance agent, investment broker, accountant or banker. Financial planning is a very specific activity and unfortunately many professionals who call themselves financial planners do not practice financial planning at all. They merely sell insurance, investments and banking products as a panacea to one's financial challenges.

While one must use these products to accumulate and protect wealth, there are several other areas that need to be addressed *before* we talk about them. So, it is then very important for a private practice owner to understand what falls under the topic of financial planning and what one should expect when working with a financial planner.

So What IS Financial Planning, Anyway?

Regardless of the individual or company you use, financial planning should always start with one thing: **a written plan.**

Here's an analogy to help explain financial planning:

Let's say that you and your spouse have finally made it to a place where your finances are in good shape, you're not worrying about bills as much, your credit is good and you even have a little in the savings account. You look at each other one day and say, "You know what, honey? Let's build our dream home." And you suddenly get all excited, start doing some research, find some interesting areas, go out and find a plot of land and say, "Okay, we're going to build a dream home. That's our plan. That's what we want to do."
So what do you do *next*? Who's the **very first person**

you talk to about building your dream home? Well, naturally, you'd go to an architect first. After all, you may have the concept in mind but you need someone with professionalism, skill and expertise to bring it to life. So you hire the architect to draw up the plans, the actual blueprint that will become the foundation for your dream home.

But that's just the beginning. A blueprint needs to be brought to life by human hands, blood, sweat and tears along with plenty of wiring, concrete and lumber. So once the plans are drawn up, then you need to hire a general contractor. Now, it's the general contractor's job to coordinate all of the subcontractors to actually build the house from the ground up.

So the contractor goes out and hires electricians, masons, carpenters and plumbers. He pulls the permits and clears all the legal, city and county hurdles to make sure that the house gets built exactly to spec. So, you have all this activity going on, sawing and nail-gunning and permit-pulling and window-installing and roofing and caulking and... what happened if you flipped the sequence?

Let's say you went out and hired the contractor first, and he went out and hired all these people, and they showed up to build your house but... the blueprints weren't done yet because you hadn't found the right architect... Could you still build a house without a blueprint?

Well, you could certainly try! The only problem is without a plan, you have no real outline for where to put the pipes for plumbing, or which walls get which outlets, or how many windows or 2 x 4's or cinder blocks. As a result, you've got all these subcontractors running around, stepping on each other's toes, working hard but doing everything out of sequence because no one knows what goes where, let alone why or how high.

And you can't have the plumber do the pipes first because, if the framing isn't done yet those pipes are going to have to come right out again, and if the electrician isn't talking to the guy who's pulling permits, then no permit gets pulled and he either can't work or has to tear out his work and start over once the permit's in place.

In short, you have this flurry of activity happening at cross-purposes because there is no central plan; there is no blueprint that says "put this here, then this here, and then this on top, and then this..." So instead of optimizing everyone's time—and your hard-earned dollars—by creating a plan first and then hiring the workers, you've got all this *non-coordination* of the subcontractors going on.

Well, financial planning is really the same way. The financial planner is really the architect; the one who writes the plan, who draws up the financial "blueprint" upon which all these activities hinge. And the "general contractor" is kind of a joint task. It is the joint task of the financial advisor and the client to work together as the general contractor.

Who are the subcontractors in this scenario? Well, the subcontractors are your specialists: your estate planning attorneys, your tax preparers and accountants, your money managers and insurance agents, your practice management consultants, your real estate agents. These are people who help you then implement your financial blueprint to get your "money house" in order.

They all do their jobs; they all have proven specialties that best fit their unique job description. The tax preparer does his thing, your real estate agent does her thing, your insurance agent does another and all those "contractors" must work together and coordinate so that they keep your best interests at heart.

How? Well, the best idea is to get them all in communication with each other as it becomes appropriate so that there is coordination of activity, and not a bunch of experts working in isolation and without any central hub and system.

What happens with most people is that they do things the exact opposite way of how they should be done. For instance, most people:

- Don't hire an architect, i.e. an actual financial planner.
- Start hiring contractors, i.e. experts, with no financial blueprint.
- Don't provide a central "hub" to allow the experts to communicate with each other.

So you've got all these people working on your behalf, but they're not creating a dream house, they're just doing so much busy work to put up a fireplace over here, and a roof that never fits, and plumbing that needs to be taken out so the framing can go in, and wires that have to be yanked out because they were installed without a permit, and stained-glass windows in all the wrong places.

You're not creating a house; you're creating rubble.

Really, really expensive rubble!

So what we're trying to do instead is get you to build a financial house in an orderly fashion so that you can build your dream home rather than just beautiful pieces of a house that never fit together properly. And that's what comprehensive financial planning is. It is hiring the architect first, then the contractors; rather than the other way around. It's providing a solid financial blueprint, or over-arching plan, around which you can create your financial dream house.

To help you in your search for your ideal financial advisor, visit econologics.com/ideal-advisor-interview-worksheet

Making Income

Goals are very important to financial planning. If you go to a financial planner from any one of a number of independent or national firms, typically they will want to know what your future financial goals are and what money you have *already* accumulated to achieve those goals. Then they will work up some analysis and specific recommendations on how to get the greatest economic benefits from the money you already have.

What's missing? **Advice on how to generate more income from your practice**!

Have you ever experienced a financial planner who consulted or assisted you on deriving more gross income or profit from your practice? Probably not. They are trained in investment and insurance management, not business consulting. However, business growth falls under the province of financial planning because to have any income at all one must **plan for it**. Your practice's viability is the major element that has to be addressed before we ever talk about investments or insurance. After all, you have to be making money to invest it!

The first area we must address when it comes to making income is your practice. That is where you spend most of your day, and probably most of your attention and energy. Why? Because your practice is the engine to your wealth!

If you don't work to maximize the value of your practice and the income that it provides you (and, by association, your household), then financial planning from that point forward becomes ineffective to the degree you have not created your wealth. Start with a solid wealth-building foundation, then work from there.

The primary consideration must be the amount of income generated by your practice (and how to increase it) and the net amount you bring home in profit (and how to increase that!). There are specific ways we go about getting positive results in this area, but are beyond the scope of this short book.

You have to walk before you can run. Likewise, income has to be earned before you can spend it. So we have to first focus on income and how to intelligently allocate the money you do make to make more money and to pay for your lifestyle, including savings. This is the basic subject of financial planning itself; it all starts with income.

One of the biggest misconceptions about financial planning is the fact that many people believe their "investment professional" will naturally make them wealthy. That is not what financial advisors do.

The only thing a financial planner can do—no matter how well-educated or sophisticated—is *preserve* your wealth. You are responsible for the level of wealth you achieve in your life and your behavior concerning what you spend, save and protect—your financial condition. A great advisor will educate you on the natural laws of money and assist you in consistently doing the right actions to achieve your goals, but it is up to you to bring those goals to fruition. Hopefully this news will empower you to see your financial planner in his or her realistic role: as consultant, not magician!

Managing Risk

After making income, the second factor we want to deal with when it comes to your practice is managing risk. What is risk? Risk is essentially the chance (or probability) of loss. These chances for loss can come in many different forms and while we can't be held prisoner to risk, we must address the reality of modern times by at least discussing risk rationally and understanding it.

You may be aware of some of the many risks that are inherent in life:

- Volatility or market risk (the values of investments going up and down).
- The risk of being sued if you are perceived to be at fault for a personal injury or damaging someone's property.
- The risks of dying too soon, becoming disabled, or getting sick can all have disastrous effects on those who depend on you.
- Or you can be negatively affected by having a loved one or a business partner die, become disabled, or get sick.
- You have longevity risk – of living too long and running out of money. Inflation risk can destroy the value of the wealth you created.
- Tax risk is in the form of ever higher taxation on income.
- Business risk in that your business is not making enough money to meet its liabilities.

- And, the risk of hiring an employee or advisor that turns out to be a huge expensive problem for you down the road.

Rather than creating money out of thin air, this is what great financial advisors do—help you identify and manage all of the risks in your financial life so you can earn more by risking less. Many financial professionals will place your accounts in different kinds of investments to diversify your risks—big companies, small companies, bonds, etc. And that is great. The only problem with this strategy is that many advisors are only managing the risks of the assets you invest with them, not for every asset in your entire household, which includes your practice and home.

Prediction

A financial plan should be able to provide you with prediction in both your income and your expenses. While it may seem like you would need a crystal ball to make such predictions, **income prediction** is actually done through a special process called "Income Planning." Prediction in expenses is easier than you think.

In truth, every future expense can be predicted, even the "unpredictable" ones. Expenses like semi-annual auto insurance premiums, tax payments and annual professional association dues are all rather easy to handle, as long as we remember to set the money aside to pay them. There are also other expenses that are more predictable than you might think.

For example, if you buy a house then you have to expect that at some point there are going to be problems with water heaters, air conditioning/heating, the roof, plumbing, and so on. Homeowner's insurance and property taxes will inevitably increase. These are predictable expenses. The fact that they occur and we don't have the money set aside for them is not an "emergency," per se, but merely indicative of a lack of financial planning. That is all.

What else can be predicted? You have a 50/50 shot of dying before your life expectancy. You have a chance of living to age 100 and will need income to support you at that age. There is a possibility that you may become ill or spend some time with a disability. Your kids may go to college. And, of course, taxes will go up.

A great financial plan will make life's ups and downs a little smoother and predictable, but only if you take risk into account and plan for it accordingly.

Efficiency

Efficiency simply means the most expedient, non-wasteful way of achieving a certain objective. Financial planning is about using the correct tools and techniques to achieve a financial objective with a minimum amount of financial risk, loss and/or waste. There is a difference between efficiency and effectiveness. For example, if you took money out of your current income and put it into savings and didn't spend that money, then you were effective in creating an asset.

However, are you being as efficient with that money as you are being effective? For instance, is the best place to keep that money in your savings account, or is there some other investment that may provide better benefits? That is efficiency. There **is** a most efficient way to achieve any financial goal you have—be that goal retirement, college education for the kids, eliminating debt, minimizing taxes, protecting your assets and expanding your practice.

Parting Words about Financial Planning

Although it can seem daunting at times, financial planning is really very simple and quite necessary. It's not just about making money; it's about putting that money to good use now and for the future.

Financial planning is all about estimating what our goals are going to cost, in advance, and save for them. So we start by setting up a special account and allocate money to it every month, while doing everything we can to protect what we have accumulated. When the time has come for that future need or goal, our savings will be there to fund it.

That's financial planning in a nutshell.

Chapter 5

The 9 Elements of a Financial Plan for a Private Practice Optometrist

While it's impossible to accurately personalize a plan just for you through the pages of this book, the goal is to create a template around which you can build a more personalized plan,

Of course, the ideal financial plan would be comprehensive and the results would be measurable. The Econologics plan concentrates on getting effective and efficient results in nine critical areas.

They are as follows:

1. A Comprehensive Written Financial Plan

It bears repeating: the plan should be written down, just like a to-do list or any other sequence of actions you want to do to accomplish something.

2. Policy and Procedure

Would you ever work for a company that did not have a policy and procedure manual? How would you ever know where you stood? These manuals exist because the company staff figured out from experience that acceptable results were achieved if you acted in a certain manner and negative results occurred if you did other actions.

Household finances work the same way. Certain actions create desirable results and other actions take you further away from your goals. If there are no written policies and procedures, how do you how to behave with your money so you can attain the financial means to achieve what is most important to you?

In a household that does not have any policy on finances, **the spouses inevitably have disagreements about money to greater or lesser degree**.

Policies are agreements made between spouses or (if single) with oneself on how different situations will be resolved.

Good examples of household economic policies could include:

- Never spending money you don't have.
- Always taking a portion of your income off the top and saving/investing it before paying anyone else.
- Having all of your financial documents organized and accessible, and so on....

Procedures are sequential actions one takes to accomplish an objective. A good example of a procedure is the annual organizing and filing of your income tax returns. If this procedure was standard and efficient, you would be saving a substantial amount of time and money each year in this area. Of course, one could establish standard, or consistent, procedures for any activity.

There are standard procedures for personal financial planning. There are many ways to go about managing your household finances, but very few ways of doing so with the highest level of efficacy. The big question is: do you know what they are? Where did you learn about personal finance and economics? School? Home? Financial guru? Or the most expensive method—the school of hard knocks? No, you were never taught about money unless you have been very fortunate to have someone in your life that mastered the subject.

Most of us are just going from one decision to another, hoping we do more right than wrong. A better idea is to get special training to learn the correct methods for each area of our financial life. This allows us to concentrate on the enjoyments of life and not the aftermaths of financial errors.

If you're going to learn the policy and procedure of personal finance, you might as well learn the simple truths.

3. Practice Viability

Is your practice financially viable? Is it expanding or contracting? Do you know how to run a business? What has been your training? Are you working with a proven practice management consultant, coach or system? Practice owners who utilize a consultant or a proven system typically have more successful practices than those who don't.

Having a calculated and rational plan is not only important for making money but for averting potential financial pitfalls in private practice. There is an extremely high cost to using the trial and error method. It is very expensive to learn that way. The investment made in a consultant to get training and practical knowledge about how to run a practice is far less expensive than the millions of dollars it would cost in lost income by "winging it" and running off the financial rails.

You worked hard to build your practice; it would be a crime to lose its benefits over bad financial planning. A private practice owner should be using benchmarks to measure his or her practice against ideal conditions.

Benchmarking your current practice condition against an optimum condition is necessary if you want to improve.

4. Planning for Income
Income Today:

Income planning is working out a plan on how much income is needed and what one intends to do to accomplish it. In planning your income today it is critically important that you focus on these major areas in your practice:

- Marketing and public relations.
- Your ability to get patient compliance and persistency.
- The quality of your treatment.
- Decreasing the cancellation rate.
- Productive personnel.

That's what creates income in a practice. You may have impeccable technical skills as an optometrist, but if you don't treat your practice as you treat your patients in regard to these criteria, you can be an excellent optometrist and still fail financially. If you're not making the income you want, then take a look at what results you're getting in any one of these areas.

For example, let's take marketing. If you can improve any area of your marketing, be it direct mail campaigns, internet presence, PR or word-of-mouth, it is going to have a positive effect on your income. If you improve all of these areas, then you will see a dramatic increase in your income.

Income Tomorrow:

Income planning also has to do with your future. Regardless of how you feel today, your interests, aptitudes and passion might change over time. For instance, there may come a time when you wish to sell your practice, or bring in other associates, or expand to multiple clinics. You may reach a point when you want to do something else with your time rather than working in the clinic full-time.

In order to free up time to do something that may not provide an income (such as traveling the world or going back to school to follow a new passion), it is necessary to be effective in not only accumulating assets while you're working, but to correctly handle a "liquidity event" such as receiving a lump sum of money for selling all or a portion of your practice or other significant assets.

The more money you accumulate and protect from adverse economic conditions such as taxes, inflation and market volatility, the more opportunity you have to use that money to create an income that can cover your expenses. Effective planning can help you determine how much income you will need in the future and how you are going to generate that income to cover whatever needs you may have at that time.

Financial planning has to do with time and money. Most people take their time and convert it into money. This may sound perfectly reasonable to you until you hear the alternative: solid financial planning enables people to take money and convert it into time. ***It is simply an equation of how much time one wants to spend earning money later in life.***

The world has changed and, with it, the amount of money we'll need well into our golden years. Many people, because they have not put anything aside, are going to be **working full-time** to create money well into their 60s, 70s and maybe even 80s. People who planned correctly and saved will be able to create time, because they will have money coming from those assets to enable them to pursue things they want to pursue, whether remunerative or not.

5. Debt and Credit Management

Where do you stand when it comes to debt and/or credit? Are you strictly against it? Or do you have a vaguely laissez-faire attitude that thinks a little is okay and a lot still isn't that bad?

Ideally, we want people to be debt free. That means living within your means and not **owing anything to anyone**. This includes getting rid of credit card and personal loan balances, operating a cash-rich practice and paying off your home (what we call "bad debt"). Loans against commercial real estate and business ventures don't really fit this definition because debt is incurred for a specific business purpose with specific economic benefits (what we call "good debt").

There are different schools of thought as to whether one should pay off their house or not. Should you? It depends.

Many financial professionals believe you should borrow against your house and invest it in assets that will potentially increase to a higher value. If you have the risk tolerance to take your home equity and speculate (i.e. you are actively willing to accept a loss in exchange of achieving a potential greater return), it may be a good strategy in certain rare cases.

Most of the time, however, if you are more conservative (that is, not willing to experience a potential loss), then paying off your house is a better idea. Your house is not an investment; it is a place to live. It does not produce income so it is not a business asset; it is a personal asset even though it may appreciate in value.

If you've decided that you are going to get out of debt, no matter how much you have, then there is a procedure to mathematically get out of debt in the quickest, most inexpensive way possible. There are thousands of ways to do it inefficiently and there is only one specific way to do it right.

6. Estate Planning

The future is never quite as far off as we think; ignoring one's future is the opposite of financial planning. Once you have had some financial success, then you need to provide financial protection for the spouse, kids, business partners, employees—everyone who is dependent upon you to generate an income—if you prematurely die, become ill or otherwise incapacitated. This is called estate planning.

Your "estate" is basically all of your "stuff," and there are probably some specific goals you want to accomplish with that stuff. But things happen and there need to be legal instructions in place to take care of these possible contingencies. Legal documents include wills, powers of attorney for healthcare decisions or legal and financial matters, living wills and different types of trusts.

Estate planning is generally neglected until one gets older (and presumably wiser) or, more commonly, an event occurs demonstrating the adverse effects of *not* having an estate plan. The people who you entrust to make decisions for you when you cannot need your guidance on how to fulfill your wishes without having to go to the courts and get permission to act.

This is inexpensive and relatively easy to do. However, if neglected, it will create more havoc and expense for your survivors than anything else in the personal finance area. While not always pleasant, no financial plan is complete unless it considers the future.

7. Tax Planning

When you earn income from any productive enterprise, your biggest creditor is the Federal Government in the form of taxation—primarily income taxation. When income is produced and profit is made, every dollar possible must go to support the goals of the household.

If only it were that easy. Unfortunately, the IRS tends to behave as if all of the money you make belongs to them. This is evidenced by the way the tax code is written: if you do nothing to attempt to reduce your taxes, you will by default pay the most possible tax you can possibly pay under current tax law for your income level.

To the degree you add more complexity into your financial life by setting up certain types of investment accounts or business structures; you may mitigate your income tax costs. Tax planning includes using the 60,000+ pages of the Internal Revenue Code to your benefit, not the other way around. Within those pages are certain code sections that we can apply as small business owners to create tax benefits.

After a while, you will experience less and less benefit for the effort expended. Theoretically, when you reach the point where the cost to implement a tax-saving strategy costs more than the taxes that will be saved, you've reached the optimum efficiency regarding tax planning.

As a small business owner, effort must be put into creating as much income tax benefit as you can for today and tomorrow. That way, the value of your hard work goes to your household rather than to the government. Who will allocate that money to its most efficient and effective use?

That's right—you will, for you understand economics better than they do.

While it may seem daunting, managing your tax expenses is critical to achieving a balance in your financial plan and effectively turning the tide away from paying the most taxes you can to the least. Again, sometimes spending less (particularly on taxes) is as good as making more money.

8. Asset Protection

You work hard, do everything right and still can lose it all, if you don't work hard to protect your assets. Asset protection is the method(s) of structuring one's affairs to limit and mitigate the chances of loss of one's assets. It is the creation of barriers between one's assets and the cause of a potential loss. Asset protection comes in many forms because losses can occur from many different sources.

One threat of loss is a lawsuit. You work in a professional capacity, so one of the problems you face is malpractice or perceived malpractice, in which someone can claim that they were injured by your actions. That is handled by setting up a business structure such as a limited liability company (LLC) or limited partnership (LP) that makes your practice more difficult to attack. One would also use professional liability insurance to protect himself. If you were to injure someone outside your capacity as a professional, there is personal liability insurance, which is most commonly found in auto and homeowners insurance.

As you can see, insurance is a great asset protection tool—it transfers the risk of loss from you to an insurance company who can financially handle the claim. Insurance can be used in many other areas to prevent catastrophic losses—life, health, long-term care, disability, property/casualty, identity theft, and so on.

Losses can occur in investments, such as declines in the stock market. If you are very aggressive and invest in start-up companies or loan money to friends, etc., there are endless opportunities for potential losses.

Inflation is another area that has to be addressed because the only value money has is its capacity to purchase things now and in the future. Losses will also occur if we do not outpace the effects of inflation with our invested assets.

Asset protection also includes areas such as taxes. These areas include tax optimization: on the accumulation of your assets, on the distribution of those assets during retirement, and on the disposition of those assets through your estate when you pass away.

What happens if you hire the wrong employee or advisor? Hiring decisions can be blissful when they payoff, and costly if a miscalculation has been made. For example, if you have ever had the experience of hiring the wrong employee and try to get rid of them only to have them come back for unemployment or worse, then you have some sense of reality around the high cost of hiring the wrong person through not only out-of-pocket costs but interference in further production. It can become incredibly expensive not to know how to hire.

Another example is spending $25,000 or $50,000 on a marketing campaign that did not pay for itself. If you've been in business long enough you've probably experienced marketing strategies that did not work. These are violations of asset protection. If you started with a $25,000 cash asset, paid for marketing and got $10,000 in value back, then that was a $15,000 loss plus the lost time and effort. These events can have a negative economic effect and need to be addressed.

So in the final analysis, if we are going to go to the expense of accumulating assets; the headache, the hard work, luck, the blood, sweat and tears, it only makes logical sense to protect those assets against loss. Only by understanding where all the potentials of loss can come from, are we then able to protect those assets.

9. Investment Management – 3 Basic Rules

Although many financial planners begin the financial planning process with a discussion about investing, investments are in fact the last financial subject in the sequence of financial planning because we must build the infrastructure of our financial life before we allocate long-term money to create assets and income in the future.

When most consumers visit a financial professional, they will address the following question and answer:

"How much money do you have? Okay, here are my recommendations for investments or insurance." Why? That's how most financial advisors get paid, whether by fees or commissions or a combination of both. The problem is that we are missing the entire spectrum of financial planning when we only look at investments and insurance as "financial planning." As we have seen throughout this chapter, that's only a small part of the overall picture.

When we talk about investments, there are three basic rules:

Rule # 1: *Profit with a Purpose*

First, when you put money away for a certain use in the future you must be very, very clear on the ultimate purpose of that money. For example, what is the purpose of individual retirement accounts (IRAs), or a 401(k), or some kind of a pension plan set up for your business? The purpose of that money is to create retirement income. Ideally, that money would generate a guaranteed lifetime income stream like the pension plan that our parents' generation had. When we invest in the IRA we must invest for that purpose and no other.

Otherwise, we will experience the tragedy of outliving the money we spent a lifetime saving.

When we decide the purpose of an investment account, there are correct ways to invest the money for that purpose and there are very incorrect ways to invest for that purpose. For example, IRAs are invested only for retirement income. They are designed to be long term programs under the tax code so we have time to invest in assets that allow us to overcome the ups and downs (if we want to speculate) or invest more conservatively to create a guaranteed lifetime income. Anything else could be either too risky or not risky enough to achieve that goal.

Rule # 2: *To Achieve a Stated Rate of Return, You Must Accept the Risk Associated with That Return*

The second rule stipulates that in order to achieve a stated rate of investment return, you must accept the risk associated with that return. Often, investments are sold on past performance and people will chase that performance considering everyone wants to make more money. The problem is the past performance is irrelevant to you unless you were actually invested in that asset over that time frame.

All investment prospectuses (the document explaining the nature and risks of an investment) must include a disclaimer that "past performance is not an indicator of future returns." But we invest anyway trying to get the previous high return, not really understanding the risks or probability of higher consistent returns that goes with that investment asset.

As the recent roller coaster ride among the stock market and economy has proven, if you want to speculate, you must be willing to accept a potential 40% loss of your money, at least for a period of time. It is an inevitable part of the game.

Do you really understand what that means? We only ask because people are doing it every single day and don't actually realize that they can lose 40% or 50% of the value of their assets by chasing "potential" higher rates of return. There is a risk for every investment you make and to appreciate that risk is a very important factor in how you will behave with your investments.

If you, as an investor, actually get excited when the stock or bond or real estate market goes down and actually look forward for these assets to depreciate in prices (so that you know you can invest more money at on-sale prices), then these speculative markets are the place for you. These would be appropriate investments, for you, because you are willing to except the risk.

However, if, when looking back to the last market bottom (circa. March 2009), you experienced any kind of negative emotion such as fear, grief, sadness, anxiety, anger or apathy because your investment values went down or you had the impulse to sell before you lost any more money, then the stock market is probably not suitable for you. This isn't a right or wrong answer; you simply have to consider your own tolerance for risk and make the right decisions for your temperament.

So often we follow the herd, or at least our friends, when what the herd does isn't necessarily what we would normally do. Financial planning is a very personal experience and shouldn't be doled out with "cookie-cutter" solutions that apply to everyone, such as with some best-selling personal finance books and TV show personalities.

To invest in the stock, bond or real estate markets (or those of any volatile assets), you must be willing and happy to accept a potential 40-50% or more downward valuation in your investments at any given time. That is called speculation. Remember, speculation by definition is the willingness to *accept a loss* in exchange for achieving a *potential* greater return; not a guaranteed rate of return.

What is the largest asset you own? Your practice (hopefully). And that is the most speculative asset you own as well. So, if you are investing in a manner that is speculative with your retirement accounts, do not be surprised if you experience wild ups and downs in the value of your assets and your emotions, because you are investing far more aggressively overall—and therefore less diversified—than you think.

Why? Because the value of your stock market investments and your practice income will both go up in a good economic environment and down in a recession or depression. This is called "correlation" and it explains why you may ride the rollercoaster of boom and bust in your personal economic condition over time. The simple correction for this phenomenon is called "diversification."

Rule # 3: *Invest to Achieve the Greatest Return for the Lowest Amount of Risk*

The third rule mandates that you should invest to achieve the greatest return for the lowest amount of risk. Tons of painstaking research has been done to prove precisely how to do that. Unfortunately, however, most investors who invest in mutual funds or individual stocks or other kinds of investments, end up taking a lot more risk than necessary to achieve desired rates of return.

A great financial advisor will assess all of your assets and show you how to allocate your money in a manner that will efficiently help you achieve your investment goals.

Your Plan to Achieve the Optimum Financial Condition

This chapter has discussed the critical areas that must be addressed by a comprehensive financial plan if you want to achieve the quality of life and standard of living you desire as a professional—and profitable—optometrist in private practice.

If each of these areas has been addressed correctly, then your household would be experiencing something closer to the Optimum Financial Condition. This would be a desirable state and would be objectively measured. It would have the following characteristics:

1. You are implementing a comprehensive written financial plan and reviewing it at least annually.

A written plan would contain programs to get each of these remaining 8 elements into excellent condition so that the prosperity of the household can be achieved and monitored without being destroyed by unpredicted losses.

The ideal financial plan would have:

- A very clear idea of the goals and purposes of the members of the household and the financial resources needed to achieve them.
- A well-defined financial condition to be achieved as a result of implementing the plan.
- No conflicting financial advice from any other advisor since only one primary financial advisor is retained.
- A firm commitment to implement the entire plan and be fully responsible for the results.
- Standard programs that are implemented to completion in the time expected.

- Results based on objective statistical measurements in the nine primary areas and not based on opinion, emotion or other subjective factors.
- The overall financial condition of the household continuing to improve on a continual basis, without losses due to errors in judgment.
- Standard annual reviews to analyze results and correction of any deficiencies found.
- Advanced planning and implementation of those strategies after basic financial rudiments are in place.
- A detailed, known and planned exit strategy, no matter how many years in the future the eventual transition out of the business may be.
- Periodic reviews of the plan being held by the Household CFO® with the members of the household on an ongoing basis.

2. Standard policies and procedures would be known and followed in the household.

This includes knowing the basics of personal finance and being competent to handle the financial affairs of the household with certainty and success (We have created a course to teach people these simple basics).

This ideal state of affairs would include:

- All decision-making members of the household thoroughly trained on the basic principles of personal financial planning and can apply them with success.

- One person in the household operating as the Household CFO who is supported by the other members of the family.
- Financial activity of the household is in alignment with workable principles, while any non-optimum behavior by any member of the household is identified and corrected.
- Money management is done standardly, saving money in appropriate accounts and keeping accurate records.
- Personal and business expenses are kept separate.
- Major financial decisions are analyzed thoroughly and are executed only when the household is in an appropriate financial condition to undertake the commitment.
- Financial mistakes and errors are avoided.
- Sources of influence that interfere with the intention to attain and maintain the Optimum Financial Condition for the household are discovered and eradicated.
- A household investment policy is written, agreed to and implemented before any investments are made.

3. You are experiencing real growth and affluence in your practice.

Your business is expanding and very profitable, allowing you time to pursue other interests in life. You are enjoying your work and are enjoying success.

The premier financial plan will have:

- The private practice owner fully trained on his or her responsibilities as a technician, executive and owner/investor.
- The practice running on a proven standard management system in which all of the staff members of the clinic agree in its application.
- The practice owner(s) trained in the subjects of strategic planning, personnel, sales and marketing, finance, organization, quality control and public relations among other executive functions.
- All staff members of the practice trained in the administrative responsibilities of their positions in addition to their technical expertise, working as team members in the expansion and profitability of the practice.
- The clinic achieving the goals and objectives as envisioned by the owner(s).
- The profit of the organization in the upper quartile of comparable professional practices in its industry while allowing the practice to operate without the direct involvement of the owner(s) for an extended period of time (at least 2 months).
- Maximum economic and social value being created in the practice for the benefit of all concerned—owners, employees, patients, community and future successors.

4. You have an abundance of income today and provisions to replace your income later in life from reserves.

You are enjoying a level of income that not only pays for your lifestyle, but enables you to set aside sufficient funds for retirement and other purposes.

In addition, the excellent financial plan would have:

- Provisions made to generate tax-advantaged income in retirement that pays for your lifestyle comfortably with the option to work or not.
- A substantial portion of household income expended each year into long-term investments, providing for known and predicted future income replacement needs.
- Analysis and provision for all "unpredictable" future expenses so no income shortfalls occur.
- Money set aside for specific goals that is never spent on another purpose than that originally determined.
- Abundant reserves accrued in investments outside the business that are protected to the highest degree possible—such as investment programs that provide guarantees of principal and income.
- Annual income on an upward trend and expanding.

5. Your household and business are completely debt-free.

Your financial plan would focus on this result as a primary action since it frees up cash flow and lowers lifetime interest costs.

The ideal financial plan would have:

- The household completely free of all consumer debt including the primary residence.
- Debt incurred by the household or any of its members only for strategic purposes such as commercial real estate, business or training uses.
- The household operates on cash for its needs.
- A first position HELOC (a Home Equity Line Of Credit—as large as possible) placed against the equity in the house to keep it liquid in case it is needed.
- The credit scores of the household over 720 FICO or 810 VantageScore, which is considered excellent credit.
- A very low utility percentage (the amount of credit used compared to the credit available) enforced by the Household CFO, keeping credit lines available but not used unless absolutely necessary.
- Accelerated debt payoff by the most efficient means available if the household began the plan in debt.
- The household not incurring total debt service in excess of 26% of gross income or residence debt service in excess of 18% of gross income.
- Consumer assets paid off as quickly as possible if borrowing was required to purchase them.

6. Your estate plan would be complete and current.

The optimum estate plan would be complete and up-to-date within the last 2 years, including:

- Current wills to determine the disposition of assets and guardianships for minor children under your directions and not the State.
- Powers-of-attorney to ensure that your health, financial and legal matters can be controlled if you are incapacitated.
- Structuring of your affairs to keep estate and gift taxes to a minimum.
- A current living will and psychiatric living will.
- Pay On Death (POD) designations on bank accounts and Transfer On Death (TOD) designations on brokerage accounts to avoid probate on such assets.
- Proper designation of beneficiaries on IRA, qualified plan, annuity and life insurance contracts.
- A properly selected and trained executor for your estate and organized files for all documents.
- The practice legally protected to benefit the decedent's heirs.
- Probate avoidance to the highest degree possible through properly established and funded revocable and irrevocable trusts, charitable planning and other strategies as advised by qualified attorneys and accountants.
- Beneficiaries who are knowledgeable of the intentions of the client so intergenerational planning can occur efficiently.

7. Your taxes would be optimized to be as low as possible for your income level.

Income taxes will always be levied against income, so a plan needs to be implemented to not only save taxes today, but for the rest of your life. Neglecting to plan for income taxes in retirement can destroy your retirement lifestyle when the time comes.

An optimized tax section of your financial plan would have:

- A condition in which one's taxes are minimized for the level of income earned even though the tax is progressive.
- The effective tax rate (amount of total tax paid as a percentage of gross household income) at the lowest possible level as allowed by law while maintaining a conservative to mildly-aggressive position as regards the tax law.
- Every deductible expense is being utilized to ultimately earn more money for the company and household, and not wasted to "save taxes."
- Basic knowledge of income tax returns and deductions known and used while questionable tactics and aggressive stances are not taken.
- Income tax rates reflect AMT (Alternative Minimum Tax) or close to it since this level of tax would demonstrate considerable tax planning and mitigation for a private practice owner.

- An annual review of tax returns—obtaining a second opinion if necessary—to potentially reduce future income tax liabilities.
- Tax-deductible interest paid if any interest paid on debts.
- Considerable attention paid to creating sources of tax-free income in retirement.
- A tax preparer who understands the needs and nuances of private practice owners in relation to comprehensive financial planning strategies.
- Advanced strategies being implemented once all basic methods are in use.

8. Virtually all of your assets have protection from loss.

This means that you own assets in a way that minimizes the risk of loss from creditors, market losses, tax losses, inflation and other forms of asset destruction.

An optimum condition for asset protection in the financial plan would have:

- The use of state statutes to protect assets like life insurance, annuities, home equity and retirement accounts.
- Business structures such as limited liability companies (LLCs), limited partnerships (LPs), and asset protection trusts (APTs) to protect business and personal assets.

- Unbundled asset structures so that income from high risk assets can be transferred to separate low risk assets.
- Proper insurances in use to protect any assets of value that cannot be easily paid for from household or business reserves.
- Competence in business management methods.
- Complete and current legal rudiments such as shareholder meeting minutes and annual reports.
- Proper use of trust strategies to create creditor-protected accounts.

9. Your investments are stable and productive.

The best investments are those that get the best results for the purpose for which they were invested. In other words, the best investment isn't the one with the highest return. If the rest of your financial plan is being done, you do not have to take unnecessary risks in any investment to become affluent—you will already be there.

The ideal financial plan for your investments would have:

- At least 6 months of living expenses in readily-accessible cash accounts.
- A substantial portion of long-term assets placed in guaranteed life insurance and annuity contracts to

provide proper diversification from the risk inherent in practice ownership.

- Investments made only in accordance with a written investment policy.
- A solid base of investment-class (principal-protected) assets established before any speculation (principal-at-risk) occurs with long-term reserves.
- A thorough understanding of the risks and costs involved with each investment before allocating money.

Parting Words about Your Financial Plan

Most people want to experience this optimum financial condition. There are a thousand different paths to get there and about a million paths that will not even get you close—you are taking a path right now, but have you asked whether that path will get you to this optimum condition that I've described here?

This is probably the first time you may have truly learned about what financial planning is, as evidenced by the fact that of the thousands of families that we've worked with over the years, almost none of them were implementing a complete plan and their results demonstrated it. This is a commentary on the current state of the financial planning profession compared to what it could and should be to a hard-working professional such as yourself.

It's time to take advantage of these tools and techniques. While they seem like common sense, they are not common knowledge. It doesn't fall down in the theory, but in the lack of implementation and action that gives us losses.

Any action taken to improve your situation, if aligned with the natural laws of economics and financial theory will improve it. Your results will tell you if your actions are the correct ones.

Chapter 6

What is Your Exit Plan?

It's always best to begin a project with the end in mind. This is true whether you're building a house or a private practice. Successful entrepreneurs always enter any venture only after they have designed an exit strategy.

Over the course of your career you are going to be spending the majority of your time working *in* and *on* your private practice. You most likely got into private practice to do things your way or control your own schedule or help others, the additional reason was that you really wanted the economic rewards of business ownership. Or else why in the world would you take all of that risk if you didn't want to have a few of the finer things?

Your practice is an investment—hopefully the largest asset you own. And someday you are going to exit that business, one way or another. The question is when, how and under what conditions you will exit. Really, there are 7 basic ways you can transition out of your practice, but for most clinic owners, they will boil down just a few—an outright sale, a management buyout (internal sale to an associate), or closing the doors.

From a financial advisor's perspective, your practice is simply one of the assets of your household and is part of your overall financial plan. While you may view it as a place to work, it is also an economic entity that provides income and has value in the marketplace. The key is to maximize the value of that entity so when the time comes for you to move onto something else—retirement, new career, etc.—you will be able to realize that value in the household so that future life goals can be more adequately funded, whatever they may be.

But here is the interesting thing: of the entire group of clinic owners we have worked with, not one of them had a written plan for exiting their practice before going through our process. We tend to be so concerned about making payroll or generating income this month that we can't put any attention on an uncertain future. The problem with short-range thinking is we don't focus on those activities that create maximum value in the practice today, and in the future we end up exiting without proper preparation, losing a fortune along the way.

According to a survey of business owners done in 2007 from ROCG, an international professional services and consulting firm, the average business owner spends 80 hours preparing a business plan and only six hours preparing for the exit. This is a tragedy considering this haphazard approach to departing your practice. In most cases, poor planning will cost six figures in value, not to mention the future income the extra money would have provide over your retirement.

The time to start planning for your exit is today, no matter if you've been in private practice for 30 years or 30 days. That's right. After all, any plan will take about 5 years to implement anyway. The first item of business is getting the practice itself structured in such a way as to maximize the financial and social value to a potential buyer. While the fundamentals of the actual sale of the practice may be worked out in 1 to 3 years, the creation of the proper financial condition for the practice and the household may take quite a bit longer.

Here are some really important things you need to know about exiting your practice:

Know exactly how you will spend your days after your practice is gone.

For the last so many years you have spent your days getting out of bed and venturing to your job, all of a sudden you wake up the day after the sale or closing of your business only to realize that you no longer have a job. This epiphany can be an exhilarating one or a terrifying one, depending on how well you planned your future life after the working years.

Probably the most important area of exit planning is how you will fill your calendar after you have sold or closed your practice. This has to do with your life's purpose and activity. Work out what your game plan is going to be regarding work, play and family before you pull the trigger on getting rid of the job. Work has a way of keeping people happy and healthy and getting out of your business may cause more problems than it solves if you don't have a plan of fulfilling life goals outside the structure to which you have been so accustomed.

You're going to spend your days doing something whether it is part-time work, leisure activities, volunteering or tackling a new career. The better idea you have of what you want that to look like, the better off you will be.

If your vision after business ownership still includes you practicing optometry (rather than pursuing another tack in life), then consider you are only burned out on managing your practice because you don't have the correct tools in place to run a business. However, if you still have a passion for being an optometrist, then practice ownership is still the key to achieving your financial goals. Get help from someone who can show you how to manage your clinic effectively as an executive.

Don't spend a dime of the proceeds until you have a written, comprehensive financial plan from a competent professional advisor.

When you sell your practice, you will experience what is called a "liquidity event" in which you take an asset that had value but wasn't liquid, your practice, and convert that value to cash. On one hand, you have secured the value of that asset into something much more conservative—cash. On the other hand, you have given up the continued cash flow from that asset and are now faced with the task of replacing that lost income into the household.

The first inclination when you receive such a windfall is to pay off those lingering credit cards, the house, or any other debt. You may even consider buying that new car or boat to reward yourself for a successful career.

Don't even think about it.

Without a well-crafted plan on how to invest the proceeds beforehand, you will likely misallocate a larger or smaller portion of that money which will lower the amount of income you will receive for the rest of your life. As a matter of fact, there have been too many instances where the seller had no plan to intelligently invest the sale proceeds and ended up broke and working as an associate in someone else's practice within five years. If you don't want this to happen to you, then work it out ***before*** the money hits your hands, not after. Without a plan, the minute the money hits your bank account, it will start disappearing at a rate that will be baffling and incredible, to say the least.

Pay off all of your personal debt before you entertain the idea of exiting the practice.

One of the financial reasons to sell a practice is to be able to take the proceeds and secure a future income without the commitment of your time and attention to create it. When you invest, you are doing so to generate a predictable income to ideally cover the cost of your lifestyle in retirement.

Any debt you have accumulated is due to purchases you have made in the past. If you take money that is designated for future income and divert it to paying off past debts, you will destroy future income potential—and lifestyle choices—to that degree.

Therefore, you want to arrange your financial plan so that you get yourself completely out of debt *before* you eliminate the income stream that you get from the clinic. Pay off everyone to whom you owe money, both personally and in the business. Doing so will allow you to increase the value and options derived from the transaction.

Have plenty of money in reserves to replace the lost income.

The most important financial question to ask in an exit plan is, "how will I replace my income?" Yes, that is the biggie. The truth is that if you expect to sell your practice and live off the proceeds without any other assets to pull income from, you will be shocked and dismayed at the results.

In general terms, you will be able to sell your practice in the 2-4 times earnings range. That means for a practice generating $100,000 a year in income and benefits, you will be able to sell it for, say, $250,000 for example. After taxes, that leaves about $200,000 to invest. At 5% per year, that provides about $20,000 a year. After adding Social Security, that leaves a shortfall of After adding Social Security, that leaves a shortfall of about $50,000 or more a year. Where will this money come from? This is called the "value gap." This income shortfall will have to be made up from going back to work or drawing income from other assets.

Can you see why financial planning is so important? It's the difference between maintaining and lowering your standard of living the rest of your life. We don't know too many people who are excited about living on less in the future.

How do you accumulate sufficient reserves to provide enough income to maintain your standard of living? Save 10-15% of your practice gross income first before you pay for any other expense for as long as you own that business. That isn't a typo. Save 10% of your Gross Income (for a clinic making $500,000 that is $50,000 saved off the top).

People delude themselves into thinking they don't need to save an adequate amount of money during the producing years to generate sufficient income during the consuming years. That's why most people are broke in retirement: not enough earned, not enough saved.

Build your advisory team before you entertain any offers.

Everyone considering an exit from their practice needs to have an advisory team. This team would include your accountant, valuation specialist, attorney, financial advisor, transition specialist (mergers and acquisitions professional or business broker), and practice management consultant. Ideally, all of the members of the team would coordinate their functions with the rest of the group to generate the best possible result for you.

The accountant will provide tax and accounting advice before, during, and after the transaction. You will want to clean up your tax returns and accounting at least two years before you sell so an accurate income and valuation can be done. Many accountants have expertise in valuing businesses, minimizing tax implications and structuring accounting systems to optimize results.

The attorney will work with you on the legal issues surrounding the sale including all of the written contracts and negotiation points. For example, when you start soliciting interest in your clinic from possible buyers, you will receive a Letter of Intent, a document stating the intent and terms under which a buyer will buy your practice. **You should never sign this document or anything else without legal counsel since these documents can become legally binding.**

Your financial advisor will be looking at the sale of the practice in the context of the effects it will have on your household and the reallocation of those assets to maximize the long-term value for achieving your life goals. He will also look at the tax implications, asset protection considerations and overall management of risk.

The mergers and acquisitions (M&A) professional or business broker will put together the deal between the buyer and the seller, ideally generating a win-win scenario for both parties. The deal structure will be worked out and agreed-upon through this person.

Within the last 5 years of your private practice, you will want to do everything you can to maximize the value of that business. To do this, you will need to be a competent executive in managing your business for growth and profit. That means getting the gross income and profitability to new highs and creating a productive staff.

The value of your clinic is only worth as much as the predictable income it will produce for the buyer. The higher the consistent and expected cash flows, the more valuable it is. The more systems you have in place and functioning, the better the deal will be.

Your test is this: if you can leave the practice for 3 months without communicating with your office staff and the income and profitability remain constant or even improve, then you have an asset worth a premium to someone else. Don't laugh, it can be done. But the way to do this is to KNOW how to do it and actually DO IT. A practice management firm that knows its business and knows your industry can help you with this.

Determine the right time to exit your practice.

How will you know when is the right time to exit your practice? This is an important question because once it's done, it's done. To be able to make this decision, it is important to break down the major factors involved.

On one hand, are you mentally ready to exit the business? Is your head still in the game or are you ready to move on? And on the other hand, is your financial house in order so that you can divest yourself of your primary income source and still pay for your lifestyle?

The decision to exit—whether you get out altogether, take on a partner, or sell to someone and work as an employee—should be worked out regarding your mental readiness to move on and your financial readiness to give up your primary income source *before* you entertain any offers or negotiations. If both of these factors are not in an optimal condition, your results will be less than optimal.

Your mental and financial readiness will give you a good starting point in the exit planning process, whether you want to get out yesterday or in 30 years. You see, if you aren't financially ready to get out but mentally ready, then you have only a couple of options: Improve your ability to manage the business and grow it (so that it is less stressful and a whole lot more fun), or sell it today at the highest price, being content with whatever you get. If you are financially ready and mentally ready, then the world is your oyster. You have the flexibility to use many different options to exit on your terms including management buy-outs, treating or consulting part-time, or planned giving strategies that provide better risk control and tax benefits.

The key to this process is to sit down and take an honest look of where you are mentally and financially. Discuss these questions with your spouse. The answers you get will help you greatly in your decision whether and under what circumstances you want to exit your practice. It can be an incredibly profitable exercise to you since it clarifies the practice's role in the accomplishment of you and your family's most important life goals. Give it the time it deserves since it probably will be the single largest business transaction you will ever make.

FREE OFFER!

Learn Your Financial Prosperity Index® Score

Congratulations, you have successfully completed reading this book, ***The Financial Success Guide for Private Practice Optometrists.*** So, what's next?

The first action one would take to put this information to good use is to get an assessment of where things stand right now; with you, your home life and, of course, your clinic.

As we studied in Chapter 2, you can't manage what you don't measure. You've already measured your practice for profitability, now it's time to turn that razor keen insight on your household!

Your household is in an economic condition—good or bad. You may have some immediate needs or longer-term concerns, but just as you do a thorough evaluation of a new patient, a financial advisor must get a thorough evaluation of your current financial health to determine what is necessary to get you in the Optimum Financial Condition. This existing condition is what it is, regardless of intentions, beliefs, current advisors, or any other factors.

This existing condition must then be compared with the optimum or ideal financial condition for your household. This has probably never been done before and is one of the critical elements missing in the entire financial planning profession. How do you know if you're on the right track if you don't have a clear idea of what would be occurring if everything was correct, completed, and tailor-made to your exact desires?

In other words, what would it look and feel like if everything was humming along smoothly and happily in your life, from a financial perspective at least? What would be in place? What would not be done? What would your daily good habits look like? Until we get a clear vision of what that "ideal picture" is for you, we have no idea if where we are is close or not close at all.

Just like every journey has a finish line, each trip has a starting line—where you are right now. A proper financial plan begins with a correct assessment of your current economic condition; this is your "starting line" for better or worse. Once all of the information is gathered, an analysis will be done to determine the correct courses of action to move you to a KNOWN and AGREED-UPON optimal financial condition. (If you don't have certainty on where the target is, the odds of "hitting it" are almost impossible).

Then policies and procedures will be written in detail to accomplish certain objectives. Implementation is the difference between a plan that is effective and or one that makes a nice coffee table decoration. Remember, big wins often pale in comparison to daily victories; these "victories" are the habitual things you do every day to court success. Making this plan, and sticking to it, will succeed or fail upon your daily habits.

In order to demonstrate the difference between a current financial condition and an optimal one, we use a tool called the Financial Prosperity Index. This tool was invented to give a professional practice owner a relative gauge as to how financially prosperous and secure his household is within the framework of our modern economic environment.

The Financial Prosperity Index uses 100 questions that reflect the basic fundamentals of any financial plan for a professional practice owner household. (For a professional associate or employee who is not a practice owner, there is also a 90-question version.) The Index is graded on a scale of 0-850 and covers all of the major areas of a complete financial plan.

For your privacy and convenience, the full questionnaire can be completed online at:

www.FinancialProsperityIndex.com

The Financial Prosperity Index graph:

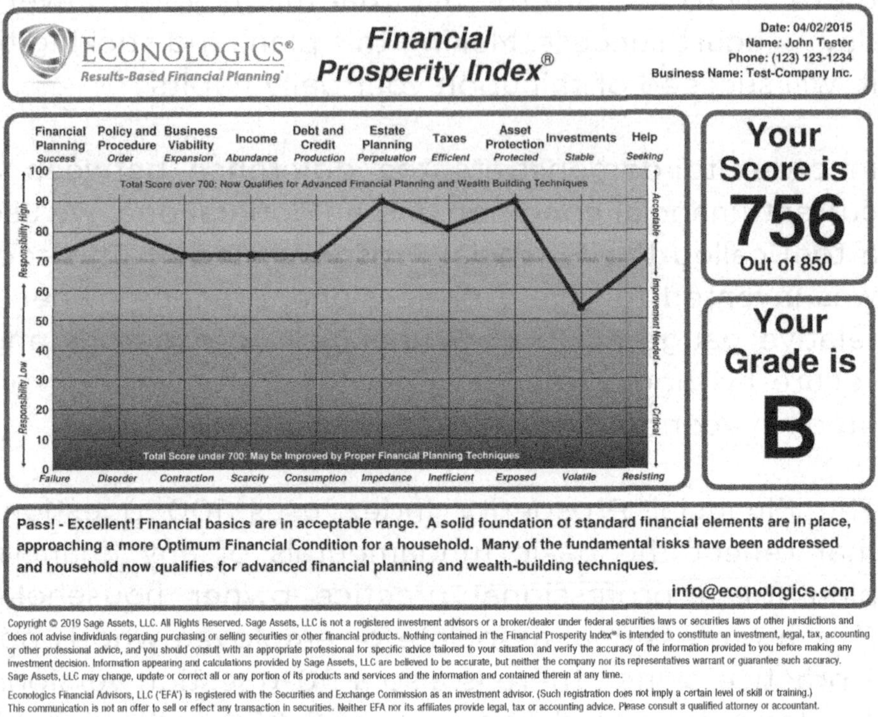

When you complete the questionnaire, please do so in its entirety. If you are married, please complete this test with your spouse and get an agreement on what the final answer should be. (It will ultimately fail if you're both not on board.) Please answer each question as to the factual truth as of today, right now, this very moment, since there will be a tendency to answer the question as you intend or **prefer it to be**. **Only an honest assessment of your present condition will give us an accurate analysis.** (It's a little like getting on the scale; holding onto the wall or leaving one foot on the ground isn't going to give you an accurate assessment of what you really weigh!)

The answers given on the questionnaire will be plotted on a graph. This graph will demonstrate the current economic condition of the household and will highlight which of the critical areas that must be addressed to improve one's financial prosperity and security. The scores are as follows:

Over 720 **Pass** — Excellent! Financial basics are in acceptable range. A solid foundation of standard financial elements is in place, approaching a more optimum financial condition for a household. Now qualifies for advanced financial planning and wealth-building techniques.

600-720 **Fair** — Several areas have exposure to loss. Many important standard financial elements are lacking, which creates substantial risk to assets. This is indicative of lack of effective financial planning and implementation—a significant divergence from an optimum financial condition for a household.

425-600 **Poor** — Massive exposure to loss of assets. Majority of financial basics not addressed sufficiently which leads to a very non-optimum financial condition for the household. Here exists an immediate critical need of proper financial planning and implementation of effective solutions.

Under 425 **Fail** — Financial emergency! This range demonstrates a real potential catastrophic loss of assets. Financial condition of the household is under duress. Most, if not all, financial basics are absent and need to be addressed and resolved. One must take corrective action immediately to salvage the economic future of the household.

Once the questionnaire is complete, a representative from Econologics Financial Advisors will contact you to set up your Financial Power Strategy Session™ and confirm a time with you and your spouse for the web meeting procedure. Both spouses must be there for the interview, as appropriate.

This is the first time that there has been an objective measurement for the results one should achieve when working with a financial advisor. This tool is part of a new subject called Econometry® Analytics. Econometry is defined as: Proprietary Analytics used to measure the economic and financial condition of an individual or a household. [<L <Gk. < *oikos* house + *nemein* to manage, <Gk. *metria* < *metron* a measure]. So, literally, it is measuring the financial management of the household by the Household CFO®.

Econometry Analytics is a set of 17 statistical tools that we use to objectively measure your household's financial condition. Just like you want to see objective results in your patients, we want to see objective results in your financial life. The value of these tools cannot be understated. Prior to Econometry Analytics, one really had no standard by which to determine whether or not one was achieving his financial objectives except by subjective means (i.e. "I like my advisor," or "we've talked about these ideas" or "he's helped me a lot") or objective measurements that were taken out of context (i.e. "I made 10% on my mutual fund last year" or "I saved $1000 in taxes").

While these measurements are important, they do not quantify your OVERALL financial condition or provide correct targets to achieve to bring about an actual prosperous and stable economic existence.

Since financial planning is an ongoing process, the goal of our firm is to continue to move you to the top of the Financial Prosperity Index graph and beyond. It does not matter where you start; just that you do, in fact, start! It simply takes the true desire and intention of improving your economic condition and implementing the recommendations fully.

The tools and techniques used in a comprehensive plan, when implemented properly, will achieve measureable improvement. It is not unlike a diet or exercise program—the program works if applied, and does not when neglected. All things worth having in life will take some effort and commitment.

Your Financial Prosperity Index will tell us what you are experiencing in your financial life and give us insight to help get you where you want to be, regardless of where that is—or how long it might take to get there.

Go to www.FinancialProsperityIndex.com TODAY and learn your score!

Summary: Your Financial Journey

Practice owners often get cookie-cutter financial advice. Instead of diagnosing specific issues, the advice from the average financial advisor is generic. The financial plan given isn't suited for the unique needs of practice ownership.

For owners, the practice is the biggest and riskiest asset, yet this is typically left out of the conversation. This is frustrating, since your personal finances should reflect the hard work you put into your practice instead of feeling like you are constantly serving your business, causing you to feel financially stuck.

You deserve to be in control of your financial future and reap the benefits of your hard work with a financial planning system designed specifically for you and your practice. No matter what phase of ownership you are in, it is essential to have a guide along this journey to navigate the business life cycle successfully.

Experience the Econologics Difference

The Econologics® Results-Based Financial Planning® System was created to help uncover the value of your practice, alleviate financial stress and put you in control of your finances so you can live life on your own terms. Your journey should include a map to know exactly where you are going and how to get there, while measuring your progress along the way to avoid financial pitfalls and mistakes so that you feel fully in control of your financial future.

We begin by helping you run your household like a business—systematized to be profitable, solvent and protected. With this mind-set, your household becomes the parent company to every other asset you own: your private practice, your real estate, retirement plans and any other businesses or valuable assets you own. This concept provides the basis for all financial planning decisions to benefit the household members and their most valued goals.

Financial Freedom Defined

Our goal is to help you achieve actual financial freedom defined as a financial condition in a household in which:

- There is sufficient income from multiple sources that cannot be outlived
- There is no bad debt
- Virtually all assets are reasonably protected from loss including taxes, inflation and lawsuits
- The business is profitable, sustainable and transferable
- And time is free to pursue other life goals

The RESULTS-BASED FINANCIAL PLANNING® System

Econologics Financial Advisors, LLC (EFA) is a full-service, Federally Registered Investment Advisor firm and licensed insurance agency providing comprehensive financial planning services nationwide using a proprietary system called Econologics®.

The team at Econologics Financial Advisors uniquely focuses solely on guiding private practice owners along their path to financial success. We understand the unique challenges of practice ownership and advise our clients on a multitude of areas such as tax minimization strategies, debt reduction, retirement and exit planning, practice expansion planning, asset protection, wealth management and so much more.

Here's how we do it:

A Clear Path to Financial Freedom

Financial planning can feel overwhelming and confusing. But that shouldn't stop you from being in control of your future. With Econologics, it's simple to gain confidence and get proven results. ***The Econologics Road Map® Financial Plan*** is a comprehensive step-by-step guide that takes the guesswork out of financial planning for a practice owner and puts you back in control. With guidance from your Econologics Financial Advisor, you will receive:

- Written Actionable Financial Plan
- Retirement Income Planning

- Debt Elimination Strategies
- Tax Optimization Blueprint
- Wealth Management
- Asset Protection & Business Structure
- Practice Appraisal
- Practice Value Drivers
- 17 Financial Metrics

Advance to the Next Level & Make Every Year Count

Circumstances and goals change over time, so planning for your future isn't a set-it and forget-it task. Keep moving forward as an Econologics Prime Client utilizing our ***Ongoing Advisory Service***. A vital part of achieving financial success is updating your plan as your empire grows. We developed the ***Econologics® Annual Road Map Renovation® Plan*** which provides you with an updated plan and new financial metrics to keep you on track. In addition, you'll have scheduled calls and ongoing interaction with your advisor to help keep you accountable for the implementation of your plan.

Exit Your Business with Ease

Deciding it's time to exit your business is a big decision and likely your largest financial transaction. Make sure you have a solid plan on how to handle taxes and income on the proceeds BEFORE you arrive at the closing table. The sale transaction can bring doubt and concern about the future, but you don't have to go into the process alone. ***The Econologics® Practice Exit & Wealth Management Plan™*** is a comprehensive step-by-step guide for owners that takes the guesswork out of tax strategies for the sale, income planning for retirement and ongoing wealth management of the proceeds.

Make Confident Financial Decisions
You probably never received a formal education on financial planning in all the years you attended school. Moreover, you want education that is simple and easy to understand—stripping away the complexities of the subject. The best way to control any situation is to first understand the subject and then apply practical solutions to get results. Get registered and attend the ***Econologics Financial Freedom Summit™***, a live event specifically designed to train practice owners how to maximize the value of their business and achieve their financial goals. Go to: www.FinancialTrainingForPracticeOwners.com

Our Team

Every practice owner needs a relationship with a financial advisor who understands the importance of including the business as a key asset in their household wealth management plan.

Our advisors will show you how to better utilize the business cash flow for the benefit of the household, guiding you through the roadblocks and obstacles of practice ownership. The end result is a practice owner's household that has achieved financial freedom and is no longer reliant on the business as their sole source of income.

Our team has guided more than 600 practice owners like you to navigate financial roadblocks and opportunities along the path of ownership. Our Results-Based Financial Planning® system helps uncover the value of your hard work, enabling you to live life on your own terms.

Take Action!

This isn't a journey you should travel alone. Get guidance and a plan built specifically for your needs so you can enjoy every phase of ownership while reaching your personal financial goals along the way.

The bottom line is you've made a number of sacrifices to get where you are and you deserve to reap the benefits of your hard work. Econologics Financial Advisors uncovers and addresses many of the major reasons why private practice owners don't meet their financial goals using our innovative, proprietary tools.

We invite you to get started on your financial journey with us with 3 easy steps.

STEP 1: ASSESS

Complete a simple questionnaire that will objectively measure and score your current financial condition and compare it to an optimum one using an easy to read graph analysis. Visit www.FinancialProsperityIndex.com to complete this assessment.

STEP 2: DISCOVER

Schedule a meeting with a specialist to review your assessment and help discover what needs to be done to improve your financial condition.

STEP 3: PLAN

Get a customized step-by-step plan from a trained, licensed advisor who specializes in working with practice owners and their families to help them reach their valued goals and continue your progress by getting ongoing guidance and accountability from your advisor to manage your progress and advance to the next level.

Visit www.EconologicsFinancialAdvisors.com for more information today!

Econologics Financial Advisors, LLC ('EFA') is registered with the Securities and Exchange Commission as an investment advisor. (Such registration does not imply a certain level of skill or training.) This communication is not an offer to sell or effect any transaction in securities. Neither EFA nor its affiliates provide legal, tax nor accounting advice. Please consult a qualified attorney or accountant.

Made in United States
North Haven, CT
10 November 2026

22091332R00065